The

Venture

Keys to Business

The

Venture

Keys to Business

By, Quentin D Williams

The Venture

Keys to Business

Contents

No Bullshit

The Venture

Keys to Business

ISBN-13: 978-1545322642

ISBN-10: 1545322643

All rights reserved. This book may not be reproduced in any way form or fashion. Unless with authors consent.

Prologue

By just reading this book isn't going to get you anywhere you have to apply what's in here to your life. You are reading this for a reason. You know what you want. Why aren't you doing it? And if you are how can you become the best at what your doing. Well where ever you stand, you are in the right place. You have been listening to a lot of stories(bullshit). This is not a story. I cut to the chase. Learn and become educated.

Pitch

The first thing people notice is the first words that come out of your mouth. This is your first impression which should be your best. This first impression should sell your product or service. This first impression should be your pitch. Do you truly know what a pitch is? Can you sell me yourself in the next 30 seconds? But a pitch doesn't just deal with the aspect of selling. A pitch also deals with the aspect of entertainment. Getting the buyer to follow you through till the end of the pitch. During your pitch you cant just sell you have to thank them for their time. They are on the phone with you or face to face with you on their own time. Make sure you thank them for that. Then engage. Start with their first name. No Mr or Mrs. Doing this makes you seem less like a salesman and like someone that person whom you are trying to sell to knows. Tell them who you are and what your business is. You can't just go to a person and tell them to buy a $100,000 bag and not tell then who you are and what you do. Telling your buyer about yourself shouldn't be more then 10 seconds. Remember you only have 30 seconds. In order for you to have the perfect pitch you have to have faith in your own product or service. You will not be able to sell anything if you do not believe in your own product or your own service. After engaging with your buyer with a brief summary about what you do. Now it's time for your pitch. The pitch is the most critical point to closing the deal. Why are you the best at what you do? Why should i pick you over everyone else who does what you do? If you are able to answer these questions, you should be fine. Now the value. What is the value of me buying your service or your product? How is your product or service going to change my life? These 2 questions if answered correctly will close a deal. In this book I don't just tell you to do things without putting it to the test. I'm going to sell you in 30 seconds.

Hi my name is Quentin Williams and I am 18 years old. I am ignorant, selfish and ruthless. And I own my own social media marketing company, which I know can help you. I am a millennial. I grew up on social media. Why have a 30-40 year old do your social media marketing? Who probably knows as much as I did when Iwas 5 years old. I can have your name on the top of Facebook, on the top of Instagram, on the top of Snapchat, on the top of YouTube even on the top of Google. I can have your name on the top of any social media out there. The world is changing from newspapers to twitter. And its changing fast. If you want your business to thrive you have to join my social media marketing program. Either you stay putting up flyers around town or have your flyer across the world.

Going live

Live is thriving. Be there or be square. Everyone is on Instagram live and Facebook live. Even the news is starting to report on things that happened on live. People want to see you. People do not want to see a recording of the old you. Now what do you do when you get on live. Pound it out man. Ask questions. Hey wassup? What do you want to know? Have the comments rolling in so fast you cant read them. Ask for them to share your live stream. People will not do what you want them to do unless you tell them. Smash the like bottom, smash the share bottom, comment questions you are dying to know.

Cold call

OTP (on the phone). Cold calling and pitching is very similar. You can't be a little bitch. You have to talk like you know your service or product is going to change their whole entire life. The first five seconds of a phone call is the most critical. Be fast. Be quick , be clean, tell the value. But in some occasions things are different. Someone might call you, but you can not close them on a deal. Look, if they call you they already know what you do. They obviously knew you were the best option. They obviously knew you were the best at what you do. So make them aware of that. Tell them that. You know now I'm the best so lets do this. Also You will never make the close on the deal if you don't ask for it.

Ads

Hey you yes you. Use anything to grab peoples attention. Some people use luxury cars in the background for peoples attention. Some people use girls, houses, celebrities, beautiful scenery. Take advantage of your surroundings. If you are on a vacation in Hawaii go ahead and record yourself at the beach. Use anything and everything to your advantage. Use it to market your product or service, use it to promote yourself. Your job as a entrepreneur is to ensure the success of your business. And without customers you do not have a business. So make ads. Its only 3 steps man.

#1 Observe where you are.

#2 How can it relate to your business.

#3 Then put it up. Its simple.

You make it hard. Oh I don't know how to make a ad. Have you looked it up on google?

Waiting

I don't understand people. I'm gonna wait till I get the money. I'm gonna what till I'm older. Use the idea that you have now and use that to build. If You are writing a book and haven't even started. Start promoting it. Hey October 6th I'm dropping a book called blah blah blah. Make a Instagram for it and make a Facebook for it.

Promote it. Have people waiting for your product or service. By doing this people around the world can give you ideas and tips on your product or service. So now whenever you drop, you can drop big. Come out of the gate making sales. You have to find your Target market. Who is your product or service for? Those should be the people who you are promoting too. How can you take the idea that you have now and start now? You never know till you try it.

Presentations

Using what I am about to tell you now can be used for big presentations or even sometimes going live on social media. What's the topic? In that one topic you should be able to pick out 4-5 subtopics. Each sub topic you should be able to talk about for hours. social media marketing, the cold call, the pitch, the close. Make it simple but be able to go in depth. At the end of the presentation, call to action. People don't know what to do unless you tell them what to do. How can a dog know when to sit if you don't tell them.

Exposure

Exposing yourself to a different area that you have not been before. You have to promote yourself. You can't just promote yourself for a day. You can't promote yourself for a week. You always have to promote yourself. You have to be as frequent as possible. People should look at you five times a day and ask them selves who is this person. They should be at the state where they want to learn more about you. Increase in contact information. Drag back to a call or the product or service. Tell people what you want them to do. Sales, just advertising is not going to cut it though. You have to be more than a product or service. You have to contact people. Touch people with your voice. Prove they should do business with you. Humanize your business.

Viewers

Views, Man I love me some views. Every view is a potential customer. They viewed you because they are interested in whatever you have to offer, or attracted to the look of your ad. Everyone already says that they know how to get views. Why aren't you making any sells then? You cant tag 100 tags on Instagram expecting to make 100 sales. You have to leverage yourself. How can you get those people to you. Positioning, find something people in your target market already know and try to position yourself as close as possible with the business or service almost like an accessory. If I do window repairs. I would go to my social media And look up houses or houses for rent. I would find the best page with the best follower base. And then contact that page. Aye man I love what you're doing with the page. Let's do a shout out for shout out. You shout me out and I shout you out, or provide value to them. It's a win win situation. Then on top of that go follow the people that's following them. Stop just existing and be known.

How to advertise in any market

You cannot sell anything or any service if you do not fully believe in your product or your service. Know what your doing and be able to produce. You have to let people know what you do. Why you? What do you produce? How do you produce it? If you are able to answer these questions sufficiently and promote them correctly. You should be able to get in any market you want.

Promote

Turn every waking moment into promoting. Your responsibility is to promote. This is who I am. This is what I'm about. Your responsibility relies on the success of your business. Which depends on how much you promote. You have to do so much it almost becomes natural. You can be talking to your friends about something and then promote your products on accident.

Cross promoting

What is cross promoting? The dictionary definition of cross promoting is cooperative and marketing of two or more companies products. You cannot be afraid to ask your competition. Shout out for shout out man. Why not. Make sure when you do this you're follower base is strong enough. Then the cross promote your products with your competition. Use this product to sell this product is all a game. LETS PLAY DAWG.

30 sec ads

Assume your audience knows nothing. You want to be big and flashy and immersive. Your ad should in case the people who watch it. Get in there. Say hi, hello. This is for you. Also you need to have good images. Ask questions for your viewers to answer. Tell them what the service or product is. Tell them who you are. Tell them the value. Tell them what makes you the best from everyone else. This should have people's hands in their pockets looking for money to give you. How can you change my life?

How to get around powerful people

How do you move to the next level? Hook up with the people who are doing what you want to do. Don't just keep yourself with one person. Go to business conventions. Go on Twitter, Instagram, Facebook and contact people. Direct message them. How do you do it, ask them that. Pump their head up. Tell them, you are coming to them because they are the best at what they do. But have other people behind you who you said the same thing too. Get as many ways to run a business as possible. Get every tip. Ask how did they get to where they are, what did they do? You need knowledge. This shouldn't take more than a week. Then make the decision to start, act, go. Go for the gusto.

Time

This is my favorite. "I don't have time". Lol. "I have to play with my toys". "I have work." If you have the time to blame time then you have time. People the problem is you don't want to make time. What is One thing in the world everyone has, time. Billionaires have time, millionaires have time, you have time. Stop telling yourself you don't have time. Stop making excuses and get it done man. work faster and produce quality work if you have to. Stop blaming time. Start making it.

Interviews

Believe it or not a interview is not about you. The interview is for the other person. It's to identify you. You have to identify why you are doing an interview. It lets the other person know how you are going to take their business in a different light. You have to navigate the interview. The person interviewing you will say, who are you? Thanks for coming. Do you have questions. Then ask the person who is interviewing you how did they get started. Start interviewing them. Show intrest in their business and watch you stand out. Become educated.

Building a personal brand

Understand that you have to have the desire. You need to realize what you want to do. You have to believe in yourself. Tell yourself that you can talk to people, tell yourself that you can promote. People have to know you. They will not know you till you talk to them. What's your brand? What does it look like? What can you offer that nobody else offers. Be obsessed. Be persistent. Ask yourself why do you do what you do. You have to build yourself. Being persistent insurers the success of your business.

Figure it out

People are filled with excuses. If you don't know how to figure something out Google it. Get I don't know out of your vocab.

Goals

Make long-term goals not short term goals. Pave your way to success. Don't make a short term goal. Because things will be shit in the long run.

Thirsty

You have two. The Internet is free. This means anyone can do anything. You have to try to put yourself out of business every day before someone else does. Never settle. Always produce.

Hate

You are going to get made fun of. Let's face it. When people see something new they automatically have their own opinion on it. But use their opinions to promote yourself. Let them tweet about you, but make sure they tag you. By tagging you and talking about you they have just promoted you. Free promotion let's get it. If you see a post about someone online, and it was bashing a person. More then likey you are going to go to the persons page they are talking about and see what they had to say or try to figure out how it started. People can not mind their own business. So when they see you have your product in hand.

How to get whatever you want.

You have to ask people if you want them to do it. Push it in their face. Tell them, I want you to buy this. If you have to hand out flyers don't ask, just hand it to them. If you want likes, ask for it. If you want to sells tell them to buy it. Either you are a spectator or a player. You are 100% responsible for everything you do. If people aren't buying, it is because of you. You are not telling them to purchase. You get what you ask for. So you have to ask for it.

What is prompting

Promotion is the ability to say what you do and what you are about. What do you create? You are trying to answer as many questions as possible. What are you promoting. Either a product or service. Promotion is an avenue for you so you can show what you do. Look for things you can talk about every day. Don't worry about running out of things to talk about, because you are always creating and your always growing.

An artist

You are a creative individual. With the responsibility of envisioning the future. You see things that aren't there. You go beyond the norm. You deserve to get paid for that.

Creative process

Lets say that you get a subject. You have to be able to get 1,000 images that relates to that subject in your head. Movies, shows, cars, buildings, weather, and people. Now you have to choose what applies best with the subject. Now you have to weave up the best. Now break it down. Get to know your viewers. Are they sad, mad, covert or an asshole? Is your ad going to be calm or harsh? Art is a way of communicating without a voice. Now, what affect do you want to leave for people. Do you want to sell or teach. Convert yourself. convert your business.

How do you know what your audience wants?

You have to be able to create a lot of content. Look at the likes and comments you get on some of the things you post. Post things that have the same characteristics of the post that has a lot of likes. Then you have to communicate with the audience. You have to know what they are thinking. Even ask them, what do you want to see more of. How can you get in direct contact with your audience? This is the best thing you can do with a new business.

Knowing what your brand is.

People say, in order for you to become big you have to have a famous person behind you or you have to have money. Or else you will not be able to make sales. The reason they are saying this is because you have not expanded enough. You have to create. You have to be seen. Be recognized. You have to be enormous. You can't be the ripples in the water. Clouded by all the noise on social media. You have to be the wave. To the point where they know when you are coming and everything stops. How do you get there though. Know who you are and know the space you are in. You have to start.

How to start content

Stop thinking you are stupid. Stop thinking your ugly. Get over that fear. Get past the haters. Then decide you really want to create. Take your highest points and make that your main focus. STOP JUST EXISTING.

Fear

You are scared to fail. You were scared your girlfriend will judge you. You are scared your friends will judge you. Worst you are scared your parents will judge you. You have to stop giving a fuck. You need to position yourself for success.

Today

You do not know how much opportunity you have. Your phone is the biggest. Your phone is your TV, News, radio, and your communication. You don't have to be rich. If you know how to use your phone, you can succeed. You can be put on the map because of your phone. You just have to know how to use it to your advantage. Stop being a viewer. Go out there and get views.

Marketing

Big companies spend almost $1 million for a TV ad. When you're watching your TV show how many times do you really watch ads, or do you go on your phone till your show comes back one? The world is changing and changing fast. Open your fucking eyes. I'm so serious. Once big corporations realize what e-commerce are doing to advertise, advertising prices on social media are going to skyrocket. Take advantage while you can.

Facebook ads

Facebook is on the top of the list for social media ads. All you need is a page and a picture or video to advertise. You can pick your target market. You can pick the price you want, as low as a $1 a day. You can pick the location you want your ad to be promoted. You need to wake up before it too late.

How not to advertise

Stop sending fucking emails. No one looks at advertised emails. Your wasting your time and money. You need to run your business like your in the 2000 not 1970. Go on social media and pay for ads. Go to Facebook, twitter, Instagram, snapchat , Google AdWords and make ads.

Knowledge

Not knowing is an unacceptable excuse. That's why we have Google. You can go on Google and type in how to do something and you will get 1 million different ways to do what you want to do. The same goes for YouTube. You are the only one that is stopping you. Be real with yourself. The only way that you're going to be able to run your own business is if you cut the bullshit with yourself.

Being wrong

Oops you made a mistake. One thing that you should be very grateful for is that you live in America. Failing in other countries is near life and death. In America you can fail and get back up. Or you can fail and do nothing about it. You have to stop thinking about your failures and get out there and keep it moving. The key to being a entrepreneur is taking risk and moving fast. Stop procrastinating. Because somebody is thinking what you were thinking and it's a race between you and them so, who is going to be the winner?

Opinions

The only reason why you are not successful right now is because of what other people think of you. What are they going to do or say that is going to change your whole entire life. Nothing. If you cut their bullshit out, and be clean, you should be ready to go. You have to realize that you have one life. Either you live your own life, or you let people tell you how to live your life.

Winner

Either you are going to read this and put all of these things into your life and become a winner. Or you're going to sit there and ponder on when you should actually start, rather then starting now. I want you to do one thing. For one week I want you to do the now Challenge. I want you to replace later with now for one week. After the week is over I want you to go back and review your week and see just how much you got done.

Average

Are you average? Well what's average? Standard, typical. Do you truly know what social media is? Social media is the social medium a.k.a. average. People go on social media to see what's going on in other peoples lives. See what's trending, what's cool. Then people buy what's cool and trending so they can become average. But to those people it's more then becoming average. It's becoming accepted. See what a lot of people fail to realize is how much things you really do for other people. Some people change there wardrobe, even the way they talk. But what about being different.

Remember this if nothing else average people get average results. But aye target those average people. Target what's trending so you can make sales. So your product can become "cool" and everyone wants it.

No one is going to hold your hand anymore. Everything you need is literally in the palm of your hand. You say you want to be successful. You say you want to be wealthy. But you don't do anything. You don't get the results that you want. It's because your not working hard enough. You're not being honest with yourself. You are underestimating yourself. Stop letting other people tell you what you can or cant do. Stop letting people live your life for you. You are part of the greatest evolution in communication man has ever seen. Don't get left behind. Get real. Get paid.

Stop

Sitting

Around

www.ingramcontent.com/pod-product-compliance
Lightning Source LLC
Chambersburg PA
CBHW061233180526
45170CB00003B/1277